About Charles River Editors

Charles River Editors was founded by Harvard and MIT alumni to provide superior editing and original writing services, with the expertise to create digital content for publishers across a vast range of subject matter. In addition to providing original digital content for third party publishers, Charles River Editors republishes civilization's greatest literary works, bringing them to a new generation via ebooks.

Introduction

Cagney in *G-Men* (1935)

James Cagney (1899-1986)

"You don't psych yourself up for these things, you do them...I'm acting for the audience, not for myself, and I do it as directly as I can." – James Cagney

A lot of ink has been spilled covering the lives of history's most influential figures, but how much of the forest is lost for the trees? In Charles River Editors' American Legends series, readers can get caught up to speed on the lives of America's most important men and women in the time it takes to finish a commute, while learning interesting facts long forgotten or never known.

When the American Film Institute assembled its top 100 actors of all time at the close of the 20th century, one of the Top 10 was James Cagney, an actor whose acting and dancing talents spawned a stage and film career that spanned over 5 decades and once compelled Orson Welles to call him "maybe the greatest actor to ever appear in front of a camera." Indeed, his portrayal of "The Man Who Owns Broadway", George M. Cohan, earned him an Academy Award in the musical *Yankee Doodle Dandy*, and as famed director Milos Forman once put it, "I think he's some kind of genius. His instinct, it's just unbelievable. I could just stay at home. One of the qualities of a brilliant actor is that things look better on the screen than the set. Jimmy has that quality."

Ultimately, it was portraying tough guys and gangsters in the 1930s that turned Cagney into a massive Hollywood star, and they were the kind of roles he was literally born to play after growing up rough in Manhattan at the turn of the 20th century. In movies like *The Public Enemy* (which included the infamous "grapefruit scene") and *White Heat*, Cagney convincingly and grippingly played criminals that brought Warner to the forefront of Hollywood and the gangster genre. Cagney also helped pave the way for younger actors in the genre, like Humphrey Bogart, and he was so good that he found himself in danger of being typecast.

While Cagney is no longer remembered as fondly or as well as Bogart, he was also crucial in helping establish the system in which actors worked as independent workers free from the constraints of studios. Refusing to be pushed around, Cagney was constantly involved in contract squabbles with Warner, and he often came out on top, bucking the conventional system that saw studios treat their stars as indentured servants who had to make several films a year.

American Legends: The Life of James Cagney examines the life and career of one of Hollywood's most iconic actors. Along with pictures of important people, places, and events, you will learn about Cagney like never before, in no time at all.

Chapter 1: From Street to Stage

"It was just everyday living. With me, it was fighting, more fighting, and more fighting. Life then was simply the way it was: ordinary, not bad, not good, just regular. No stress, no strain. Of course, no one had much of anything but we didn't know that we were poor." – James Cagney

On July 17, 1899, James Cagney was born on the tough streets of the Lower East Side of Manhattan, and at the time his family was so poor that they didn't bother keeping careful records of family births and addresses, so the actual location of his birthplace remains a mystery. His father, James Francis Cagney, worked any job he could find and was, at one time or another, a bartender, a boxer and (at the time of his second son's birth) a telegraphist. Cagney's mother, Carolyn, was a first generation American with roots in Ireland and Norway, and it was from her that Cagney inherited his red hair, blue eyes and hot temper.

Cagney was the second of seven children, but two of Cagney's siblings died within months of their birth, which the family attributed to their poverty. As Cagney put it in his own autobiography, there was almost a third: "I was a very sick infant. My mother, only 20 – a mere child herself – was terribly worried, of course. What bothered her most, next to my possible demise, was the fact that I hadn't been baptized. As a good Catholic, she felt that if I were to die before I was given a proper name, I'd never be allowed into heaven. She bemoaned this again and again to her brother: 'He hasn't got the name – he has to have a name!' Now, my uncle was a pretty rough Irishman. He humored her for a while, but Mom continued to cry the house down about my lack of identity. Finally he turned on her and said, 'Carrie, for God's sake, shut up! Stop your crying and call the kid Ikey!" At that time, the Lower East side was characterized more than anything else by its diversity, ensuring Cagney grew up surrounded by people who had come to America from all over the world. He would later be grateful for this type of upbringing, noting, "The polyglot nature of my neighborhood is the basic reason why all my life I've had such an appreciation and understanding for dialects. I ought to – I was surrounded by them. Indeed, I was 22 before I ever heard an elderly man who spoke without an accent…"

Like most living in the heart of New York City at that time, the young boy always had a job. At one time, it was as an office boy for the *New York Sun* making $5 a week, all of which he gave to his mother. Later, he worked at the New York Public Library for $12.50 a month. He also played semi-pro baseball and he was so good at amateur boxing that he once finished runner-up for the lightweight boxing title in New York State. He wanted to turn professional, but his mother warned him he would have to beat her first, so he soon gave up the idea. Cagney later recounted his time working as a young kid positively, explaining, "It was good for me. I feel sorry for the kid who has too cushy a time of it. Suddenly he has to come face-to-face with the realities of life without any mama or papa to do his thinking for him."

After it was clear he wasn't going to be a boxer, Jimmy next turned to a less suitable but more lucrative line of work: serving as a maître d' at an upscale tea room. His job at the tea room may seem strange, considering Cagney's tough guy image, but he was certainly more rounded than the average street tough. In addition to boxing and playing baseball, he also took tap dancing lessons, and friends that knew him as a young man recall him as "Cellar Door Cagney" thanks to the knack he had for dancing up the side of slanted cellar doors.

Nor was young Jimmy Cagney all brawn and no brain. After graduating from Stuyvesant High School in 1918, Cagney enrolled in Columbia University as an art major, but by this time, the United States had entered World War I. Assuming that the war would go on for a number of years, and already having an ear for German gained as a child, Cagney also decided to major in the language. This immediately benefited him when it came to joining the Student Army Training Corps, a predecessor of the Army ROTC, and Cagney might have gone on to a career in the military had fate not intervened. The war ended in November 1918, and an influenza pandemic swept through the world, taking the life of his father and leaving his mother a young widow pregnant with her seventh child. This sudden turn of events forced Cagney to drop out of school and move home to help make ends meet.

Thankfully, Jimmy Cagney had some sort of photographic memory, which not only helped him excel in school but also opened the door for his acting career. Like so many other would-be actors, his interest in performing began with the movies. Cagney's aunt lived in Brooklyn near the Vitagraph Studios, and while visiting her, Cagney would hang over the edge of the fence surrounding the studios and watch movies being filmed, especially those involving his favorite actor, John Bunny.

John Bunny

Eventually, Jimmy would follow his older brother Henry into the amateur dramatic club at the Lenox Hill Neighborhood House, where he worked primarily behind the scenes as a stagehand. At the time, the younger Cagney had no interest in acting, but that all changed one night when Harry became too ill to carry on with his part. The director, Florence James, called on Jimmy to take his brother's place, and because of his excellent memory, Jimmy had no problems learning the script. He went on stage that night with the lines memorized and mimicked his brother's acting movements, which he had remembered from watching rehearsals. Naturally, the applause from the audience proved to be a thrill for him and left him wanting more.

Chapter 2: The Boxer Who Danced

"You know, the period of World War I and the Roaring Twenties were really just about the same as today. You worked, and you made a living if you could, and you tried to make the best of things. For an actor or a dancer, it was no different then than today. It was a struggle." – James Cagney

Jimmy might have been bitten by the acting bug, but playing bit parts in dramatic companies was not going to pay the bills, so he also got a full-time job at Wanamaker's Department Store in 1919. Undeterred, he was still working there when he auditioned for a small part in *Every Sailor*, a war time musical with a chorus made up of service men dressed as women. He later explained the unusual nature of this first part: "And that is how I began to learn dancing, as a chorus girl. I faked it to begin with. I would stand in the entrance, catch the real dancers, and steal their steps. Thereafter, in all the dancing shows and acts I did, I learned by watching." While it would certainly surprise many to hear that the classic Hollywood tough guy played his first part in drag, it didn't faze Cagney at all because when he was acting, "I am not myself. I am not that fellow, Jim Cagney, at all. I certainly lost all consciousness of him when I put on skirts, wigs, make-up, powder, feathers and bangles." It certainly didn't hurt that they were paying Cagney $35 a week, which he considered "a mountain of money for me in those worrisome days."

Though Carrie was proud of her second son's success, she still wanted him to return to college and get a degree. He refused to go back, but he did leave the department store and take a position as a runner for a local Broad Street brokerage house, and in his off time, he continued to audition, eventually getting a part in the chorus of *Pitter Patter*. He was paid over $50 a week, but he sent $40 of it to his mother. More accustomed to hard work than the life of an actor, Cagney also made additional money by working as a dresser and carrying luggage for the other actors. The show proved to be Cagney's first part in vaudeville.

While working on the ticker counter, Cagney met Frances Willard "Billie" Vernon, a 16-year-old member of the female chorus line, and they soon fell in love and married in 1922. They then moved into a sort of early style of commune called Free Acres that was established in Berkeley Heights, New Jersey. Cagney and his wife would tour together with an act called "Vernon & Ide", and later, he would replace Archie Leach, of the Parker, Brandon and Leach act. The name Archie Leach doesn't mean much to anyone anymore because Leach later changed his name to Cary Grant.

Cary Grant

Cagney and his wife with actors Jack Oakie and Joan Marsh

In 1924, Vernon and Cagney moved across the country to Hawthorne, California to try to break into the movies, even though they were so poor at that time that they had to borrow the train fare from a friend who was also an aspiring actor. At first, Cagney tried to support himself and his wife by teaching dancing, but perhaps not surprisingly, there were already plenty of dance schools near them and thus not enough clients. Cagney was unable to make ends meet, forcing the couple to give up on their dream of making it out West. They borrowed more money to move back to New York. These were obviously hard times, and Jimmy never forgot them, or what it took for them to make it through. More than 50 years later, he would give his wife the credit, saying "the rock solid honesty and the sterling character of this little gal made it possible our going comparatively unscathed through the years when we were in dire straits. And when I say dire straits, I mean 'dire' and I mean 'straits.' It was rough. At times no food in the larder, big holes in the shoes. When I didn't have a penny, she was out working. Life seemed just a never ending sequence of damned dingy, badly furnished rooms with a one burner plate. There were many times when I was sorely tried and decided to get out of the acting business, to go out and get any kind of job that would bring in the weekly paycheck. But every time I mentioned it, my Bill told me with pleasant firmness, no."

Fortunately, Cagney fared better on the stage than he did in the movies. In 1925, he was cast as a tough guy in the play *Outside Looking In*, and his work in that production earned him a far more comfortable living at $200 a week. Since he had no experience doing dramatic acting, Cagney later admitted he thought he got the part because his hair was redder than that of the other performer he was competing against, but regardless, the play was popular and garnered Cagney a number of positive reviews. One critic in *Life* magazine noted, "Mr. Cagney, in a less spectacular role makes a few minutes silence during his mock-trial scene something that many a more established actor might watch with profit". Burns Mantle, a stage critic who founded and wrote for *Best Plays*, claimed *Outside Looking In* "contained the most honest acting now to be seen in New York."

However, Cagney faced another major setback in 1926, when he was promised but then lost a part in George Abbott's Broadway. Believing that they would be sailing to England to perform the show in London's West End, Jimmy and Billie had their luggage loaded on to a ship and had given up the lease on their apartment, but the day before they were to leave, Cagney was told that he no longer had the part. Cagney's wife later recalled that after this turn of events, "Jimmy said that it was all over. He made up his mind that he would get a job doing something else."

That something else turned out to be something familiar. To make ends meet, Cagney tried his hand again at teaching dance, and this time, his students were fellow professionals, so he was able to make more money. More importantly, he was also able to hear about new plays opening, which is how he secured a role in *Women Go on Forever*. For four months, Cagney taught dance all day, and danced across the stage all night. By the time the play ended, he was both physically and mentally exhausted.

The following year, Cagney was cast in *Grand Street Follies of 1928*, and this time, he was also made the choreographer. The Follies were a hit, which led to the reprisal of the show the following year as the aptly named *Grand Street Follies of 1929*. In vaudeville, as in life, Cagney soon learned that nothing succeeds like success; his successful roles in the Follies led to a part in *Maggie the Magnificent*. Though the critics didn't much care for the play, they praised Cagney's performance, and Cagney praised director George Kelly for his professionalism: "On *Maggie the Magnificent*'s first day of rehearsal, he said to us, 'Now, boys and girls, we have hired you because we know you were experienced. I will benefit of all that experience. We think you know your business. Anything that occurs to you, please let me know – because I can't think of everything. So – if you would do me the favor of speaking up? All right now, let's get to work.' Naturally, with such a complete professional in control, there was no need for us to give him anything." Cagney also said he learned "what a director was for and what a director could do. They were directors who could play all the parts in the play better than the actors cast for them."

Chapter 3: The Public Enemy Becomes a Public Hero

"Though I soon became typecast in Hollywood as a gangster and hoodlum, I was originally a dancer, an Irish hoofer, trained in vaudeville tap dance. I always leapt at the opportunity to dance films later on." – James Cagney

Following *Maggie the Magnificent*, Cagney and his co-star Joan Blondell were cast in a new play called *Penny Arcade*. As with the previous play, the critics did not like *Penny Arcade*, but they loved Cagney and Blondell, and when Al Jolson saw the couple's talent, he bought the rights to the play for $20,000 and then turned around and sold the play to Warner Bros., with the caveat that they would hire Cagney and Blondell to re-create their parts on screen. Warner Bros. cast the two, giving Cagney a three week contract for $1500 to play tough guy Harry Delano, and this type of part would prove to be his bread and butter for the rest of his career. Despite the fact it was his first film, Cagney refused to be cowed into doing stuff he didn't like, including a scene he wouldn't shoot: "There was a line in the show where I was supposed to be crying on my mother's breast...'I'm your baby, ain't I?' I refused to say it. Adolfi said 'I'm going to tell Zanuck.' I said 'I don't give a s*** what you tell him, I'm not going to say that line.'" By holding firm, Cagney had the line removed from the script.

Joan Blondell

The film adaptation of *Penny Arcade*, titled *Sinners' Holiday*, was released in 1930, but Cagney's on screen career began not so much with a bang but with a whimper. The studio liked him, but they weren't sure how much they liked him. Thus, when the shooting ended, Warner offered him a seven-year contract for salary of $400 a week, but the studio added an unusual stipulation that specified it could drop him at the end of any 40 week period. In other words, Cagney could find himself out of work after any 40 week period, but since he had no better offers and still needed to support his family, he took the contract. When looking at Cagney's decision sign with Warner Bros., it's essential to keep in mind his background. $400 a week was a substantial amount of money for a family that had grown up broke, and by this time, the stock market had crashed and many Americans had no work at all. At the time, getting paid $400 a week to stand in front of the camera was easy money in his mind, though he would soon change his mind.

Cagney's next picture was *Doorway to Hell*, and it was followed by several other gangster films, including *Little Caesar*, in which he played opposite Edward G Robinson for the first time. Over the next few years, these two men would come to define what it meant to be a gangster in a Hollywood film. But ultimately, Cagney's big break became in 1931 when he was cast in *The Public Enemy*. The very nature of the casting for that film is the stuff of Hollywood legend, as Cagney would later recall: "Then came *The Public Enemy*. The story is about two street pals – one soft-spoken, the other a really tough little article. For some incredible reason, I was cast as the quiet one; and Eddie Woods, a fine actor but a boy of genial background, well-spoken and well-educated, became the tough guy. Fortunately, Bill Wellman, the director, had seen *Doorway to Hell*, and he quickly became aware of the obvious casting error. He knew at once that I can project that direct gutter quality, so Eddie and I switched roles after Wellman made an issue of it with Darryl Zanuck."

Robinson in *Little Caesar*

Wellman clearly made the right decision, because *The Public Enemy* soon became one of the first films to ever gross more than $1 million. Not only did the public love the movie, the critics loved it. A reviewer in the *New York Herald* said that Cagney's performance was "the most ruthless, unsentimental appraisal of the meanness of a petty killer the cinema has yet devised." Some critics have cited the film as changing the way that the public would perceive good guys versus bad guys, asserting that Cagney's portrayal of Tom Powers as a murderer with a heart of gold introduced the genre to Hollywood. However, Cagney always disagreed, pointing instead to Clark Gable in *Night Nurse* as being the first "good bad guy".

The movie attempted to be so realistic that Cagney was actually punched in the face in one scene, and another called for him to duck from live gunfire, but the most famous scene in the movie comes when Cagney's character angrily picks up half of a grapefruit and shoves it into his girlfriend's (played by Mae Clarke) face. The shocking nature of the scene, and the surprise on Clarke's face, led many to assume that it was an impromptu move on either Cagney's part of the director's part, and that Clarke wasn't told what was coming her way. For her part, Clarke claimed that she knew the grapefruit was coming, but that she had been told it wouldn't actually be included in the movie itself: "I'm sorry I ever agreed to do the grapefruit bit. I never dreamed it would be shown in the movie. Director Bill Wellman thought of the idea suddenly. It wasn't even written into the script." Even today, movie experts refer to it as one of the most significant moments in film history, and naturally, Cagney had his own take on the issue: "When Mae Clarke and I played the grapefruit scene, we had no idea that it would create such a stir...I was not to hear the end of that little episode for years. Invariably whenever I went into a restaurant, there was always some wag having the waiter bring me a tray of grapefruit. It got to be awfully tiresome, although it never stopped me from eating it in the proper amount at the proper time."

Cagney was glad to have work, and he appreciated the money he was making, but he was still the scrappy tough guy from the Lower East Side who refused to be pushed around by anyone. For instance, when Douglas Fairbanks, Jr. organized a charity drive, the studio insisted that every actor participate, but Cagney refused, saying that while he was glad to donate to charity, he would not be forced to do it. This incident and subsequent others would eventually earn him the title "The Professional Againster" in Hollywood.

While shooting *The Public Enemy*, Cagney was also working with Edward Robinson on *Smart Money*. Warner liked the way the two men interacted on screen, so the studio wanted them to get back together in another film as soon as possible. In spite of the fact that he had never hit a woman in real life, Cagney was once again called upon to assault his leading lady in *Smart Money*. This time, he had to slap his co-star, Evelyn Knapp. However, things were changing in Hollywood at the beginning of the 1930s, as motion pictures, once considered a novelty, were becoming more mainstream in American society. With that came an outcry from conservative Americans and religious groups to limit the amount of sex and violence in pictures. Needless to say, they did not appreciate films in which men assaulted women, and they also didn't like criminals being portrayed as having redeeming qualities. Warner decided to take Cagney's career in another direction by casting him with Joan Blondell in a comedy, *Blonde Crazy*, but this new direction wouldn't last long.

Chapter 4: Working For and Against Warner Bros.

"There were many tough guys to play in the scripts that Warner kept assigning me. Each of my subsequent roles in the hoodlum genre offered the opportunity to inject something new, which I always tried to do. One could be funny, and the next one flat. Some roles were mean, and others were meaner." – James Cagney

The Public Enemy was so popular that movie theaters were running the movie 24 hours a day just to keep up with demand; in fact, one legendary anecdote about the movie related by Cagney is that Joan Blondell's ex-husband figured out the times the grapefruit scene would be on and would duck into the theater to catch it as often as possible. Given the movie's popularity, Cagney realized that he was bringing in a lot of money for Warner Bros. but was not being paid as much as many of the other actors whose films were not doing as well. He approached the executives at the company and demanded a raise, and when they refused and also insisted that he spend his extra time promoting other films, Cagney quit, turned his apartment in Hollywood over to his brother Bill, and moved back to New York. He would describe his rationale for this move: "The trouble surfaced when I realized that there were roughly two classes of stars at Warner's: those getting $125,000 a picture – and yours sincerely, who was getting all of $400 a week. That $400 soon stopped because I walked."

While it was obviously a risky decision, it was also a wise one, because the popularity of *The Public Enemy* and *Blonde Crazy* had the public clamoring to see more of him. While Jimmy was gone, his brother was able to persuade Warner to renew his contract and pay him $1000 a week, after which Cagney returned to Hollywood and began working on *Taxi*. This film marked both a first and a last in his career. The first was his dancing, as he performed an excellent number on screen for the first time. The last was getting shot at with live ammunition. At the time, studios regularly shot at their actors with live rounds because blanks were considered too expensive, and Cagney had taken it for granted that it was part of the job. However, during the filming of *Taxi*, something happened that changed his mind: "…one of the machine-gun bullets hit the head of one of the spikes holding the backing planks together. It ricocheted and went tearing through the set, smacked through a sound booth, ripped across the stage, hit a clothes tree, and dropped into the pocket of someone's coat." From that point forward, Cagney refused to put himself in the line of fire, and that decision may have saved his life on the set of *Angels with Dirty Faces* because an errant bullet passed through the place where he would have otherwise been standing.

The film *Taxi* also contains one of the most misquoted lines in movie history. At one point in time, Cagney yells at his enemy, "Come out and take it, you dirty, yellow-bellied rat, or I'll give it to you through the door!" For some reason, this line began to be quoted all over the nation as, "MMMmmm, you dirty rat!" To this day, impressionists still use it when impersonating Cagney.

Warner may have thought that they had won the battle with Cagney over his salary, but they were wrong. Cagney returned to Hollywood for $1000 a week, but he believed that his work was worth $4000 a week, which is what Edward G. Robinson and other actors of the era were making. Cagney again demanded a raise and again threatened to quit if he did not get it, but this time, the studio called his bluff and suspended him. Cagney responded that if that was their attitude, he would quit acting altogether and return to Columbia University to become a doctor. Finally, after six months of wrestling, Frank Capra was able to persuade Cagney to accept $3000 per week, along with top billing and the assurance that he would have to film no more than four movies a year. This success would lead to Cagney becoming one of the leading members of the Screen Actors Guild when it was founded in 1933.

1933 and 1934 had Cagney making multiple movies for Warner Bros., and as is usually the case, some were better received than others. *Footlight Parade* was particularly popular, and Cagney enjoyed making it because it allowed him to sing and dance on stage again. The dance sequences, choreographed by the famous Busby Berkeley, are considered some of the best of the era. Cagney's other favorite movie of that time was *Here Comes the Navy*, not so much because of the quality of the film but because he got to work with Pat O'Brien, who would become one of his best friends. Ironically, the movie was filmed aboard the USS *Arizona*, several years before it would be sunk by the Japanese at Pearl Harbor.

Cagney and Blondell in *Footlight Parade*

Cagney and Gloria Stuart in *Here Comes the Navy*

By 1935, Cagney was considered one of the 10 biggest moneymakers in Hollywood, but when asked if this was the big moment when he realized he was a star, he replied with his usual honesty: "Nothing of the sort! I never gave it a thought, never thought of it at all. Whatever was going on in my Hollywood life I regarded as completely transitory. I looked on it only as doing a job, and that job happened to work out. And the answer to all this is, where did I go nights? I sure wasn't going around picking up the kudos – or the kiddos. I just stayed home."

Cagney finally got to be on the other side of the cops and robbers game in *G-Men*, this time playing an FBI agent tracking down a wanted criminal. After that, he made his first and only foray into Shakespeare by portraying Nick Bottom in *A Midsummer's Night's Dream*. Needless to say, he would not try such a role again.

Instead, Cagney next made a third film with Pat O'Brien, this one called *Ceiling Zero*, but in this film, Warner again challenged Cagney's contract. First, they listed O'Brien above him in the credits, a clear violation of his top billing clause, and the company had already pushed Cagney by having him make five movies in 1934, another violation. He had let this pass, but the billing issue proved to be the final straw. He sued the studio for breach of contract, and after again leaving Bill to handle his professional and business matters, he returned to New York. When looking at his contract battle with Warner, particularly his preference to renegotiate over and over again, it may seem that Cagney was stubbornly insistent on having his way at all costs, but he cast his actions in a different light: "Top billing is an entitlement that means money in the bank, and I was protecting my entitlement. I walked out because I depended on the studio heads to keep their word on this, that, or other promise, and when the promise was not kept, my only recourse was to deprive them of my services. I'd go back east and stay on my farm until I had some kind of understanding. I'm glad to say I never walked out in the middle of a picture, the usual procedure when an actor wanted a raise."

Back in New York, Cagney began shopping around for property outside the city and claiming that he would just settle down to farm. Though he grew up in the city, Cagney had been interested in farming ever since his mother took him to hear a talk on soil conservation when he was a young man. Thus, while he was off from work, he purchased his first farm. Located on Martha's Vineyard, it consisted of 100 acres of bucolic quiet, but his wife didn't care for the place at first; Billie was concerned about the money and work it would take to make the deteriorated old house and out buildings habitable. Jimmy persisted, however, and she soon came to love it too. For his part, Carney maintained that the Vineyard "represented for me the place where I could always go to find freedom and peace…"

Of course, the Cagney's would have to work hard to maintain their peace, especially after Jimmy's fans learned where they lived. In order to avoid multiple strangers showing up at his door, Cagney spread the rumor around the area that he had hired an armed guard to patrol the place. This led to a comical situation when his pal Spencer Tracy came to visit. Tracy's cabbie would not pull up on to the property, explaining to him "I hear they shoot!" Thus, Tracy had to walk up the dirt road on foot to get to the house.

Jimmy Cagney the actor might have disappeared altogether and been permanently replaced by Jimmy Cagney the gentleman farmer had it not been for Edward L. Alperson, who represented Grand National Films, a new studio that offered Cagney $100,000 per film plus 10% of whatever the movies made. Cagney accepted this deal and returned to Hollywood to make *Great Guy* and *Something to Think About* for Grand National. These movies are unique among his performances of that era in that he plays a more sympathetic "good guy" rather than a criminal, but while his performances were critically acclaimed, the movies themselves were low-budget and looked it. Grand National ran out of money before it could make any more films, and Cagney once more found himself looking for a new project.

Cagney did not have to look for long; he won his case against Warner Bros., setting a new precedent for actors who had formally been bound by the studio system. More than that, the studio actually invited him to return to work for them, this time offering him a contract for $150,000 per film, with a clause guaranteeing that he would have to make no more than two movies each year. He could also choose which pictures he made. Always a family man, Jimmy insisted that his brother Bill be made the assistant producer of any movies he was cast in.

Cagney's victory against Warner Bros. proved to be a triumph in the politics of Hollywood, and it also led him to become involved in other political matters, a decision that would later cause him some problems. In 1936, the specter of war was consuming Europe, with Hitler and the Nazis in Germany and Mussolini rattling his saber in Italy. The world was watching, and though most Americans were still isolationists, Cagney believed that the Nazis needed to be stopped. As a result, he joined the Hollywood anti-Nazi League, unaware that the League was actually a Communist front. This would come back to haunt him later.

In the meantime, Cagney was back working for Warner Bros. After working with Pat O'Brien in *Boy Meets Girl* in 1938, Cagney teamed up with him again in the classic *Angels with Dirty Faces*. Cagney had had his eye on this role for some time and had hoped to make it for Grand National. In it, he stars as recently released gangster Rocky Sullivan, and while trying to track down an old pal who owes him money (played by Humphrey Bogart), Sullivan runs into another old friend, Jerry Connolly. Played by O'Brien, Connolly is now a priest working with at-risk kids, many of whom idolize Rocky. He tries to persuade Sullivan to go straight but fails, and Sullivan ends up being sentenced to the electric chair.

Cagney and O'Brien in *Angels with Dirty Faces*

In the moments leading up to his execution, Connolly visits Sullivan and pleads with him to "turn yellow", so that the kids who have so admired him will lose their respect for him and his criminal ways. Sullivan refuses to humiliate himself and insists that he will walk to the chair like a man. However, at the last moment, he falls to his knees before his executioners and pleads for his life. For years, critics would speculate over whether Sullivan's seeming cowardice at the last minute was a real last ditch attempt to save his life or feigned to appease Connolly, but Cagney would never say: "Through the years I have actually had little kids come up to me on the street and ask, 'Didya' do it for the father?' I think in looking at the film it is virtually impossible to say which course Rocky took – which is just the way I wanted it. I played it with deliberate ambiguity so that the spectator can take his choice. It seems to me it works out fine in either case. You have to decide."

Critics hailed Cagney's performance in *Angels with Dirty Faces* as one of his best, and he received his first Oscar nomination for Best Actor, but he ultimately lost out to Spencer Tracy, who ironically won it for playing a priest in *Boys Town*. However, Cagney did snag the coveted New York Film Critics Circle award for best actor, and it would hardly be his last Academy Award nomination.

By 1939, hard work and a hard-nosed approach to business had made Cagney the studio's highest paid actor. In fact, his annual salary of $350,000 was second only to Cary Grant's in the entire industry. While Warner probably didn't appreciate the route Cagney took to get to that position, the studio also knew it was money well spent. Cagney finished up the year with *The Roaring Twenties*, his last film with Bogart and the last gangster movie he would make for a decade. As usual, he received good reviews, with Graham Greene remarking, "Mr. Cagney, of the bull-calf brow, is as always a superb and witty actor".

Cagney with Bogart and Jeffrey Lynn in *The Roaring Twenties*

The Roaring Twenties marked the end of another era for Cagney, although this time the change was more subtle. As noted earlier, Hollywood was under increasing scrutiny for the moral message of its films, and during the 1930s, most of Cagney's gangster characters were portrayed as having turned to a life of crime because of being raised in abusive and/or poor environments. As the 1940s dawned, public perspective was shifting, and from this time on, large-scale violence was seen as part of a mental illness or, at the very least, a lack of self-control.

Chapter 5: Yankee Doodle Dandy

Cagney in *Yankee Doodle Dandy*

By 1941, Jimmy and Billie Cagney had been married almost 20 years, but they still had no children, so they decided to adopt an infant boy whom they named James Cagney, Jr. A few years later, they would adopt a girl and name her Cathleen. Tragically, while Jimmy and Billie remained close throughout their marriage, they had a difficult relationship with their children. James Jr. died two years before his father following a long period in which the two were estranged, and Cathleen would remain estranged from her father until his death.

Jimmy Cagney is best known for playing gangsters with one notable exception: his portrayal of George M. Cohan in *Yankee Doodle Dandy*. Both critics and Cagney himself believed it was his best role ever, and there are a number of reasons (in addition to Cagney's talent) *Yankee Doodle Dandy* was such a hit. One is that the crew began filming the picture on December 8, 1941, the day after the bombing of Pearl Harbor, so it goes without saying that everyone working on the project was in a state of what one person called "patriotic frenzy." Cagney's co-star, Rosemary DeCamp, noted the cast and crew had a feeling that "they might be sending the last message from the free world" out to the country. At the premiere, the company sold seats for up to

$25,000 each, donating the money to the U.S. Treasury in the form of war bonds, and in that one evening they raised almost $6 million for the war effort.

Another factor that made the film a hit involved the parallels between Cohan's and Cagney's lives. Both men got their start in vaudeville, they both struggled hard before finding success, they both were devoted to their families, and they had both been married to the same women for many years, which was no small feat in Hollywood then (or now).

Cohan

Both the public and the critics loved the movie. *Time* wrote, "*Yankee Doodle Dandy* (Warner) is possibly the most genial screen biography ever made. Few films have bestowed such loving care on any hero as this one does on beaming, buoyant, wry-mouthed George M. (for Michael) Cohan. The result is a nostalgic, accurate re-creation of a historic era of U.S. show business." As far as Cagney's performance was concerned, they were equally enthusiastic, noting, "Smart, alert, hard-headed, Cagney is as typically American as Cohan himself... It was a remarkable performance, probably Cagney's best, and it makes Yankee Doodle a dandy." Perhaps the biggest praise came from Cohan himself; when he saw Cagney's performance in the film he exclaimed, "My God, what an act to follow!"

Of course, one of the reasons Cagney succeeded in the role was the very reason he was cast for it: "Psychologically I needed no preparation for Yankee Doodle Dandy, or professionally either. I didn't have to pretend to be a song-and-dance man. I was one…In just about every interview, in most conversations, one question emerges unfailingly: what is my favorite picture?…A discerning critic like Peter Bogdonovich can't understand why I choose *Yankee Doodle Dandy*…The answer is simple…Once a song-and-dance man, always a song-and-dance man. In that brief statement, you have my life story: those few words tells as much about me professionally as there is to tell….Its story abounds in all the elements necessary for a good piece of entertainment. It has solid laughs [and] great music. And how much more meaningful are those patriotic songs today in view of all our current national troubles! *Yankee Doodle Dandy* has lots of reasons to be my favorite picture." When Cagney wrote those words in 1974, the troubles he referred to were very different than those faced at the time of the film's release, but *Yankee Doodle Dandy* stood the test of time. Even today, it remains an American favorite.

Not surprisingly, considering the both the nature of the film and the year in which it was released, *Yankee Doodle Dandy* was nominated for eight Academy Awards. It won three, including Cagney's win for Best Actor. When accepting his award, he remained humble, saying, "I've always maintained that in this business, you're only as good as the other fellow thinks you are. It's nice to know that you people thought I did a good job. And don't forget that it was a good part, too."

Following his success with *Yankee Doodle Dandy*, Cagney teamed up with his brother Bill to create Cagney Productions, and their plan was to make movies themselves and then release them through United Artists. However, Cagney was in no hurry to get back to work; instead, he returned to his farm on Martha's Vineyard to rest up. After that, with the war still ongoing, he joined the United Service Organizations (USO) and began touring military bases and visiting soldiers. At each base, he would recreate scenes from *Yankee Doodle Dandy*, as well as some of his early song and dance work.

In September 1942, Cagney returned to Hollywood and was elected as president of the Screen Actors Guild. The following year, Cagney Productions released its first film, *Johnny Come Lately*, starring Cagney as a newspaperman in the late 19th century. According to Cagney, "…our biggest accomplishment in *Johnny Come Lately* was to establish as one of the hallmarks of Cagney Productions the liberal use of good supporting actors. As Time magazine said about this, 'Bit players who have tried creditably for years to walk in shoes that pinched them show themselves in this picture as the very competent actors they always were. There has seldom been as good a cinematic gallery of U.S. small-town types.'"

Jimmy and his brother took a real chance with *Johnny Come Lately* because most of the larger studios were focusing on making war films, and that's what the American public seemed to want. While the film did receive some positive reviews and made a reasonable amount of money, it was not the type of hit Cagney was used to making. Thus, instead of beginning to work on another film right away, he went on another USO tour, this time to England.

Cagney enjoyed his time in England and worked hard to entertain the troops stationed on military bases there. He often gave multiple performances in a single day of his main act, "The American Cavalcade of Dance", a history of dance in 20th century America, and finishing with numbers from Yankee Doodle Dandy. The only thing that Cagney wouldn't do was give interviews to reporters covering the tour; when some British reporters approached him one time, he responded, "I'm here to dance a few jigs, sing a few songs, say hello to the boys, and that's all."

When Cagney came home, he quickly got to work on Cagney Productions' next film, *Blood in the Sun*. Always willing to try something new, Jimmy trained with martial arts expert Ken Kuniyuki and a former policeman named Jack Halloran to do his own stunts in the film. After the failure of *Johnny Come Lately*, the brothers hoped that the spy thriller set in Japan would be more appealing to American audiences. However, while *Blood in the Sun* was popular with critics and even won an Academy Award for Best Art Direction, it was a box office failure. Compounding that failure, Cagney had spotted a photo of a young war hero named Audie Murphy and believed that Murphy had the looks and poise to make it in pictures, so he invited him to Hollywood for a screen test. Unfortunately, Cagney didn't recognize the acting talent of the future actor and thus sold his contract to another company shortly after.

While trying to line up the rights for Cagney Productions' third movie, Cagney starred in *13 Rue Madeleine*, a spy picture that paid him $300,000. The film was a success, and Cagney used the money he made to produce *The Time of Your Life*, an adaptation of the Broadway play by the same name that appealed to critics but not to audiences. The problem was not Cagney's acting ability but the unwillingness of the public to accept him in the role of Joseph T., a quiet, philosophical people watcher.

During the years following World War II, Cagney became increasingly active in local and national political circles, an interest that had been sparked in the 1930s when he opposed the "Merriam Tax," a form of "under the table" bribes given by studios to the campaign of Frank Merriam, California's candidate for governor. Each actor was expected to donate a day's pay to Merriam's campaign, but out of principle, Cagney not only refused to make the required contribution, he also threatened to donate a week's salary to Merriam's opponent.

At first, Cagney considered himself to be a political liberal, and he supported Franklin Roosevelt's election and policies. He was also involved in what he later described as a "liberal group...with a leftist slant". However, when another member, future president Ronald Reagan, warned him about the direction the group was taking, he and Reagan resigned. Furthermore, his one-time involvement in the Anti-Nazi League caused him problems as the Red Scare and Cold War became everyday facts of life in post-war America, but thankfully he was ultimately cleared by the notorious House Un-American Activities Committee.

Furthermore, while serving as the president of the Screen Actors Guild in 1942 and 1943,

Cagney led the Guild's opposition to the Mafia. There had been rumors for years about a group affectionately dubbed the "Irish Mafia" that Cagney himself was allegedly a member of, consisting of a group of Irish-American actors that like to get together for dinner and drinks, but by the early 1940s, Cagney found himself up against the real thing, an organized crime family that wanted to get their cut of the Hollywood action. Unlike many of his fellow actors, Cagney has seen guys like these before, and even after his wife got a call telling her that she was now a widow, he was unperturbed. When they stepped up their threats by hiring a hit man, Cagney contacted his friend George Raft, who apparently had his own underworld ties. He "made a call", and the hit was called off.

While Cagney had liked Roosevelt, he was not as fond of Harry Truman, so in 1948 he voted for a Republican candidate (Thomas E. Dewey) for the first time in his life. The next two decades saw him become firmly entrenched as a conservative, and Cagney explained this transition in his autobiography: "I believe in my bones that my going from the liberal stance to the conservative was a totally natural reaction once I began to see undisciplined elements in our country stimulating a breakdown of our system. From what I've seen of the liberal attitudes toward the young and the permissive attitude in the schools and everybody pulling every which way from center, I consider these all inimical to the health of our nation. Those functionless creatures, the hippies, for example, just didn't appear out of a vacuum."

Chapter 6: Mr. Cagney Meets Mr. Roberts

"Made it ma! Top of the world!" – Cagney's character in *White Heat*

The string of failed pictures left Cagney's own production company in deep debt, so Cagney made a deal to return to Warner Bros. with his company coming in as part of the deal, and the first picture made under the new agreement was *White Heat* in 1949. Unlike his previous characters, many of whom seemed to have a good reason for killing, Cagney's character (Cody Jarrett) was the mentally ill son of a man who had died in an insane asylum. He also had serious mother issues, even sitting in his elderly mother's lap at times. Not surprisingly, he dies a dramatic death at the end, killed in a massive explosion after gunning down some of his own men and shouting one of the most famous final quotes in a movie, "Made it ma! Top of the world!".

Cagney in *White Heat*

The studio called the movie the story of a "homicidal paranoiac with a mother fixation", and Cagney didn't disappoint. His performance in *White Heat* is considered one of his best, and in one of the most famous scenes, he did an impromptu take in the scene where Jarrett learns of the death of his mother that fellow actors didn't know was coming. His portrayal was so realistic and terrifying that it frightened some of his fellow cast members. The critics and the public both loved *White Heat*, but Cagney wasn't as happy with it. In spite of being America's "Yankee Doodle Dandy," he was still struggling against his gangster archetype, and by this time he was also the father of young children. As such, he told one reporter, "It's what the people want me to do. Someday, though, I'd like to make another movie that kids could go and see."

Cagney and Virginia Mayo in *White Heat*

In light of these feelings, it's no surprise that he jumped at the chance to star in another musical, this time opposite one of his favorite leading ladies, Doris Day. The musical was called *The West Point Story*, and Cagney said of it in his autobiography, "There was some critical thinking and hollering about the key plot line: the assignment of a Broadway musical director to actually live the life of a West Point cadet for some weeks. Such a thing just couldn't happen, some critics said. Only it did. Both Westbrook Pedlar and George M. Cohan did just that at various times."

However, Cagney's next film, *Kiss Tomorrow Goodbye*, brought him back to portraying a gangster, mostly because Cagney Productions, which had been purchased by Warner Bros., was deeply in debt. Having been raised to always pay his own bills, Cagney would not declare bankruptcy, and he insisted on making and marketing *Kiss Tomorrow Goodbye* to make money. Though the critics did not care for it, the public did, and they bought enough tickets to pay off Cagney's creditors. The company made just one more film, *A Lion is in the Streets*, and then shut down.

Cagney particularly enjoyed his next role as Martin "Moe the Gimp" Snyder in the 1955 movie *Love Me or Leave Me*, which he called "that extremely rare thing, the perfect script." Doris Day played his wife, Ruth Etting, in this biographical piece, and since Snyder was Jewish, it allowed Cagney to use the accent he had mastered when he was growing up on the Lower East Side. He also mastered Martin's limp to such an extent that Snyder himself asked Cagney how he did it. Cagney simply replied, "What I did was very simple. I just slapped my foot down as I turned it out while walking. That's all." Critics loved the film, and Cagney was nominated for another

Academy Award. He certainly would've won is the award was chosen by co-star Doris Day, who called Cagney "the most professional actor I've ever known. He was always 'real'. I simply forgot we were making a picture. His eyes would actually fill up when we were working on a tender scene. And you never needed drops to make your eyes shine when Jimmy was on the set."

Doris Day

Cagney in *Love Me Or Leave Me*

Next, Cagney worked with legendary director John Ford on *What Price Glory?*, but Cagney was not crazy about working with the famous director because Ford insisted the film be shot as a regular picture rather than the musical Cagney had signed on to make. Cagney would later refer to Ford having a "slightly sadistic sense of humor," which included allowing him and another actor to be injured in a motorcycle collision on set. The two nearly came to blows, as Cagney later recounted, "I would have kicked his brains out. He was so goddamned mean to everybody. He was truly a nasty old man." On another occasion, as Ford yelled at him, Cagney got back in his face, "When I started this picture, you said that we would tangle asses before this was over. I'm ready now – are you?" After that, Ford finally backed down.

John Ford

Given his dislike of Ford, it is somewhat surprising that Cagney agreed to make his next picture, *Mister Roberts*, with him, but Cagney wanted to work with his friend Spencer Tracy, who was supposed to play opposite him in the film. It was only after he had agreed to make the movie that Tracy was replaced by Henry Fonda, but he enjoyed working with Jack Lemmon, whom he described as "a nice young fella". In his autobiography, Cagney recalled the following story:

"I realized that upcoming was a scene with Jack, as Ensign Pulver, that I'd found so funny in the reading that I realized it would be marvelously so in the playing. The difficulty was that it was so funny I had serious doubts about my ability to play it with a straight face. I talked it over with Jack. I said, 'We've got some work ahead of us. You and I'll have to get together and rehearse that scene again and again and again until I don't think it's funny anymore.' He agreed because he had the same feeling about the scene. So we got together and did it and did it and did it. But every time I came to the payoff line in the scene, 'Fourteen months, sir,' I just couldn't keep a straight face. Finally, with enough rehearsal we thought we had it licked. We came to filming time.

"....This is one hell of a funny little scene: the commanding officer of a naval vessel finally meeting an ensign who had been ducking him during their voyage for well over a year. I used to collapse every time Jack said 'Fourteen months, sir,' but when we filmed it, I was able to hang on just barely. What you see in the film is the top of Mount Everest for us after our rigorous rehearsals. It still kills me every time I think about it."

Cagney wasn't the only one who thought the scene (and the entire film) was hilarious. The movie received three Oscar nominations, including one for Best Supporting Actor for that "nice young fella," Lemmon.

Chapter 7: The Gangster Goes Straight

"The last curtain call is usually the best. When it's time to go, you should go." – James Cagney

Following the completion of *Mister Roberts*, Cagney bought a new 120 acre farm in Dutchess County, New York. He named it Verney farm and poured tremendous effort into making it a working business, and over time, he bought more of the surrounding property, growing the farm to 750 acres. His agricultural efforts earned him an honorary degree from Rollins College in Florida, but rather than just accept the award, he insisted on submitting a paper on soil conservation to justify receiving his degree.

One feature that all Cagney's farms had in common were their horses. When Cagney was born in 1899, horses were still the primary mode of transportation in America, and as a city boy, his family obviously owned no horses, but he always jumped at the chance to get to sit on the back of the nag that pulled the milk truck. As an adult, he enjoyed buying, breeding, raising, training, and talking about horses, and Giant Morgans, of the big feet, were his favorite breed.

By this time, Cagney was 56 years old but still going strong both physically and mentally. He made his next movie, *Tribute to a Bad Man*, for MGM. This film, one of his few Westerns, had actually been written for Spencer Tracy, but Tracy was unable to complete filming due to health issues, so Cagney took over. *Tribute to a Bad Man* did well at the box office, leading MGM to cast Cagney opposite Barbara Stanwyck in *These Wilder Years*. Cagney liked Stanwyck from their time together in vaudeville years earlier, and in an off-screen scene reminiscent of something out of the movies, the two old stars entertained their younger cast members with song-and-dance numbers from their youth.

Stanwyck

Unlike many of his counterparts, Cagney had no interest in appearing on television, but in 1956, he agreed to appear in *Soldiers From the War Returning* as a favor to his old friend, Robert Montgomery. Montgomery had his own series and needed a powerful performance to open the new season with, but when reporters cornered him with questions about future television appearances, Cagney made his position clear: "I do enough work in movies. This is a high-tension business. I have tremendous admiration for the people who go through this sort of thing every week, but it's not for me."

Having had success with several other biographical films, Cagney portrayed famous actor Lon Cheney in *Man of 1000 Faces*, and the critics ate his performance up, with one reporter calling it one of the best performances of his career. It also did well at the box office, earning a good return for its production company, Universal Studios.

During this era, it was common for well-seasoned actors to try their hand at directing, so in

1957, Cagney made his first and only venture behind the camera to shoot *Shortcut to Hell*. A remake of 1941's *This Gun For Hire*, the movie was based on the novel *A Gun For Sale* by Graham Greene. At first, Cagney believed that he would be a very effective director; when he made the movie for his friend, producer A.C. Lyles, he did it as a favor, and for his own enjoyment, refusing to be paid. This appealed to Lyles, since he had very little money invested in the picture, which Cagney was able to shoot in just 20 days. He would later say that 20 days as a director was plenty for him, remarking, "We shot it in twenty days, and that was long enough for me. I find directing a bore, I have no desire to tell other people their business".

Over the next few years, Cagney made a few other movies, and by this time, he had enough money and prestige to be picky about what he wanted to do, so these roles were some of his best. He was happy to play the role of the labor leader in *Never Steal Anything Small*. In this musical, one of the last he would ever make, he enjoyed a hilarious song and dance number with Cara Williams, who portrayed his girlfriend in the film.

After *Never Steal Anything Small*, Cagney took off and flew to Ireland, where he filmed *Shake Hands with the Devil* with the well-known English director Michael Anderson. Cagney's reasoning for playing an Irish Republican army officer was more personal than professional; for one thing, Cagney felt he could use some of his off time in Ireland to trace his family's roots. Also, he was increasingly concerned about the level of violence spreading in the country, and he was attracted to *Shake Hands with the Devil*'s anti-violence message. The critics loved the film, and many considered it one of the best performances of his final years of acting.

In 1960, Cagney brought his production company out of mothballs to produce *The Gallant Hours*, and critics loved his portrayal of Adm. William F "Bull" Halsey, who led the Guadalcanal campaign in the Pacific. Though the film was set during World War II, it was not a classic war movie but more of a psychological thriller, with the focus being on the impact of command on Halsey himself. Critics loved the movie, with one reporter saying, "It is Mr. Cagney's performance, controlled to the last detail, that gives life and strong, heroic stature to the principal figure in the film. There is no braggadocio in it, no straining for bold or sharp effects. It is one of the quietest, most reflective, subtlest jobs that Mr. Cagney has ever done."

Cagney's final career film prior to retirement was the comedy *One, Two, Three*. Director Billie Wilder insisted that he was the only one to play an ambitious, overworked Coca-Cola executive trying to establish a presence in West Berlin. While the film itself was funny, Cagney's experience in making it was nothing to laugh about. He was the consummate professional and accustomed to working with tight scripts and well-rehearsed actors, so when one scene took 50 takes to get right, he was at his wit's end. He also complained about one of his co-stars, "I never had the slightest difficulty with a fellow actor. Not until *One, Two, Three*. In that picture, Horst Buchholz tried all sorts of scene-stealing didoes. I came close to knocking him on his ass." For the first time in his long career, he actually considered walking out on the movie, but he stuck it out and completed the film. During his time on set, he also made a visit to the Dachau concentration camp on one of his days off, which made a lasting impact on his life.

Cagney retired after returning to America, and unlike many men who have enjoyed fame and success, Cagney relished retirement. He spent most of his time on his farms, with occasional trips to both coasts to go sailing. Though he often struggled with seasickness, Cagney was an avid sailor, and he kept seaworthy craft on both the West and East Coast so he could sail whenever he got the chance.

Cagney also took up painting during his retirement, and to improve, he took instructions from the famous Sergei Bongart, who later asserted Cagney was so talented he could have been a professional artist had he started younger. He even proudly displayed two of Cagney's works in his own home, but Cagney always admitted he was nothing more than an amateur and refused to sell any of his work. The only exception was one painting, which he sold to Johnny Carson for charity.

When not painting, sailing or farming, Jimmy and Billie Cagney spent time in New York, where they enjoyed hosting parties at a little place called the Silver Horn restaurant. Over time, they became close friends with the owner, Marge Zimmerman, and later, when Cagney's health began to fail because of diabetes, Zimmerman became a valued friend and caretaker for the couple. She took it upon herself to refine recipes and cook dishes that helped Cagney manage both his diabetes and his cholesterol, which was also out of control. Under her careful care, Cagney lost weight and became healthier than he had been in years.

In 1974, Cagney made a rare public appearance to accept an American Film Institute Lifetime Achievement Award. Charlton Heston hosted the event, Frank Sinatra introduced Cagney, and so many stars showed up for the ceremony that one reporter quipped that if a bomb should go off in the building, the movie industry in America would be over. For his part, Cagney had fun at the ceremony, teasing impressionist Frank Gorshin by saying, "Oh, Frankie, just in passing, I never said 'MMMMmmmm, you dirty rat!' What I actually did say was 'Judy, Judy, Judy!'". Cagney's joke was a reference to another popular misquote of him, that one being attributed to Cary Grant.

A few years later, in 1977, Cagney had a small stroke, and though he recovered, he was no longer able to enjoy many of the physical sports that he had in the past, including dancing, which he had done to keep fit, and horseback riding, which he enjoyed for the thrill. He also became depressed and gave up painting. Zimmerman and Billie both devoted all their efforts to caring for and encouraging him, with the former becoming their full-time companion, and together, the two women persuaded Cagney to come out of retirement for one role, the small but critical part of New York Police Commissioner Rhinelander Waldo in the film version of the novel *Ragtime*.

Ironically, this American classic was shot in London, and since he never liked flying, Cagney traveled to England on a cruise, the *QEII*. When he arrived at Southampton, the cruise line officials were shocked to find their honored guest and most important passenger mauled by hundreds of fans. While Cagney's performance in *Ragtime* was strong, his co-stars had some problems; seasoned but younger actors missed their cues and forgot their lines in the face of the legend. One of them, Howard E. Rollins, Jr., recalled, "I was frightened to meet Mr. Cagney. I asked him how to die in front of the camera. He said 'Just die!' It worked. Who would know more about dying than him?" Rollins' reference to Cagney's many death scenes as a gangster aside, Cagney enjoyed playing the part, and in spite of increasing back pain, he remained on set after he was done filming to help the younger actors learn their lines.

In spite of his failing health, Cagney remained a star right up until the end of his life. When he and Pat O'Brien showed up at the Queen Mother's birthday performance at the London Palladium, the monarch rose to her feet at their entrance, the only time she stood up during the entire performance. A few years later, Cagney, now wheelchair-bound, appeared on television in *Terrible Joe Moran*, the story of an aging retired boxer. In flashback scenes, the director was able to make use of some of Cagney's early boxing footage in 1932's *Winner Take All*.

Terrible Joe Moran would be his final appearance, because Cagney died two years later on Easter Sunday morning of 1986 at his Dutchess County farm. His funeral mass was held at St. Frances de Sales Roman Catholic Church, with sitting president and old friend Ronald Reagan delivering the eulogy. Afterward, his body was buried at Hawthorne, New York's Cemetery of the Gate of Heaven.

Fittingly, Cagney wrote his own eulogy via the end of his autobiography, and as was his habit, he was more interested in talking about others than himself; in this case, he told his fans, "Thanks, too, for buying the ticket that gave me this lovely and deeply loved farm whence these words come. And, above all, the very numbers of those tickets prompt me to say: grateful thanks for giving a song and dance man across the years all those heartwarming encores."

Bibliography

Bergman, Andrew. James Cagney : The Pictorial Treasury of Film Stars (1974)

Cagney, James. Cagney by Cagney (2010)

Clinch, Minty. James Cagney (1982)

Federal Bureau of Investigations. James Cagney - The FBI Files (2012)

McCabe, John. Cagney (2013)

Schickel, Richard. James Cagney, A Life In Film (Movie Greats) (2012)

James Cagney: Paperback Book (Applause Legends) (2000)

Warren, Doug. James Cagney: The Authorized Biography (1983)

Printed in Great Britain
by Amazon.co.uk, Ltd.,
Marston Gate.